201

Ways to
Manage
Your Time
Better

A Quick-Tip Survival Guide

ALAN AXELROD & JIM HOLTJE

MJF BOOKS
NEW YORK

Published by MJF Books
Fine Communications
Two Lincoln Square
60 West 66th Street
New York, NY 10023

201 Ways to Manage Your Time Better
LC Control Number 01-130245
ISBN 1-56731-464-3

Manufactured in the United States of America on acid-free paper ∞

MJF Books and the MJF colophon are trademarks of Fine Creative Media, Inc.

BG   10 9   8 7 6 5   4   3   2   1

CONTENTS

QUICK START

The folks flipping burgers at the fast-food joint are the last of the 9-to-5ers. The forty-hour week? In your dreams. Try *sixty hours*. Minimum.

Hours. There aren't enough of them. Succeeding in business has always been a tough go. These days, it's downright brutal. What do you need most?

All the help you can get.

What do you need even more?

Time.

The Quick-Tip Survival Guides put the two together, giving you all the help you need—without taking all the time you have.

Here is a series for today's business reader. A reader pressed by a hundred demands and pulled in a dozen directions. (Business as usual!) A reader whose day shoots by in milliseconds, who consumes information by the megabyte, and who cannot afford the luxury of climbing the learning curve with the leisurely aid of traditional narrative prose.

Here is a series for today's business reader negotiating today's learning curve. Focusing on the personal and interpersonal skills crucial to working successfully with customers, colleagues, subordinates, and supervisors, the Quick-Tip Survival Guides mine and refine the nuggets of essential business know-how: the time-tested truths, together with savvy from the cutting-edge.

201 Ways to Manage Your Time Better is not a tome on management and efficiency theory, but a compact quick-read collection of practical tips and easy steps that will start saving you time today. It's a book of real-world ideas for people who want—and need—to make the most out of every business day.

ARE YOU EFFICIENT? BE HONEST NOW!

1. Don't you just hate the perfect people who have their act together? They're the ones who show up at meetings a "fashionable" two minutes early, and know just when to leave. They never forget an appointment, a client's birthday, or miss a deadline. Their desks are neat, and their files in working order. To add insult to injury, they usually breeze through the day with the greatest of ease. Before you gnaw through your pencil, realize this: You can become one of them. And maybe, just maybe that's why you've bought this book.

2. Whoever first said "the best place to begin is at the beginning" uttered a profound truth. Ask yourself this question: "Are you efficient?" If you have trouble with specifics, write a list. No one else has to see it, so don't worry about revealing too much. Divide the page in half. In the lefthand column, write tasks you ordinarily perform during a typical day. In the righthand column, assess how well you do them. For example: "Finishing projects on time/I usually only finish the projects I'm interested in first, then get around to the others." Good, good, keep going. An honest start. This will help you create a road map for the rest of the way.

3. If you work for a large enough company, you are likely to be subject to performance reviews. Before you start reciting chapter and verse about how unfair your last review was, at least consider the possibility that there might be a kernel of truth in what was said. Instead of focusing on isolated points, look for patterns that reveal something about you and your efficiency. Reviews offer a third-party snapshot of how you work. Learn from them, even if you don't agree with everything that's said.

4. Can't get anything constructive out of your last performance review? Maybe you were completely snowballed, and you know you're better than the boss says you are. Perhaps it would be more useful to confide in a friend at work. Ask him or her discreetly what they think about your performance on a particular task. The trick, though, is to ask in such a way that you don't come off as eagerly trolling the waters for compliments. Try something like: "Hey, Bob, do you have a second? Listen, I really need your honest opinion about how I handled the Anderson account. If I'm ever going to work on that new project with you, I need to know that I've mastered the basics." These types of questions are especially good when they are directed at more experienced individuals who relish the role of mentor.

5. Keeping time sheets or using a computer program that tracks the hours you spend on specific tasks is a concrete method of gauging your efficiency. Say you've spent eight hours on a relatively mundane project that should have been done in no time, and yet, in that same month, you spent only three hours on a project that is critical both to your career and to the company. Einstein told us that time is relative. Who are we to argue with Einstein? But that eight hours spent on easy tasks is still five hours more than you spent on the really important work. Discover the crucial patterns by studying time sheets from several months.

6. How much free time do you have? If you're constantly bringing home work, you're either just extremely busy, or not terribly efficient during working hours. Perhaps a bit of both. If you find you're constantly lugging computer disks home to work on projects, it may be a sign that you're not using your work time to maximum efficiency.

7. What is it about others? Do you have colleagues who seem always to get their work done on time and are always efficient? What is it about their work habits that makes this possible? Do they get to work early? Do they take work home with them? Do they take shorter lunch breaks? Write down for yourself what you feel may give them a decisive advantage. Study the list. Is it a case of apples and oranges? Or is there really something you should be doing differently?

8. If you don't already plan out your day ahead of time, try this: Start in the morning by making a schedule of what you have to accomplish before leaving the office. Write down how long you think it should take to complete each individual task. Don't cheat! As you go through the day, mark down the start and stop times for each task. How did you do? Did some tasks take longer than expected? This is a sign that there may be a better way to get the task done. You just haven't thought of it yet.

9. A high-tech version of the same exercise is to use your contact manager PC or Mac program. Set start and stop points for each task. You can set the alarm on your program to sound when it's time to start wrapping things up. Be sure to record how you well you keep to your original schedule as you go through each task.

10. Preserve a record of all of your starts and stops. No, you don't have to publish it on the World Wide Web for everyone to see, but it's important for you to diagnose exactly what the problem is before you try to solve it. Keep a file at home if you're worried about someone reading it at work. The important thing, as the Oracle of Delphi proclaimed, is to "Know Thyself." And remember, if you're cheating at this stage, it's only another sign that you've got a ways to go before you're really efficient.

HOW TO START YOUR MORNING

11. What you do *before* you head for the office can have a significant impact on your day. If possible, do not use the morning to hammer out family disputes—or to hammer on members of your family. Do use the morning as a time for pleasant conversation, preferably with your family gathered at the breakfast table. If you are inclined to exercise, morning is a great time for it. An invigorating run or walk is a terrific way to start your day, and the fact is that you will find it difficult to be intellectually and emotionally fit if you aren't reasonably physically fit as well. If you aren't accustomed to exercising, don't rush into a gung-ho program. Start gradually.

12. Maybe you really love your work. But you have trouble starting your business day. If so, you are not alone. What will get you past the morning's inertia? One of the best ways to get started is to focus on what you'll do for the rest of the day. Start by working out a plan. Would you start a journey without a road map? Of course not. The journey through your day should not begin without one, either. Write down on paper, or on your computer, what you must accomplish that day. Draw up a checklist. Now, if you have trouble doing this, chances are that the stumbling block is some task you'd simply rather not acknowledge. Ignoring it won't make it go away. Start writing.

13. Check your mail, voice mail, faxes, and e-mail early. You may need to respond to someone right away, but, even more important, getting back to correspondents as soon as possible shows you're on the job. It also allows you to plan the rest of your day more efficiently. It makes no sense to write out a plan at 8:45, check your voice mail at 11:00, and then have to reschedule the rest of your day because of an urgent message you neglected earlier.

14. Schedule your meetings and lunch appointments early in the day. If you have to meet someone that day, but have not set up the time and place, the earlier you do this the better. If you know your appointment is in her office before 9 a.m., call her. You're more likely to talk to her directly, and less likely to become the unwilling passenger on a grand tour through voice mail Oz.

15. Breakfast meetings are an excellent way to steal time from an otherwise overbooked day. They allow you get work done before the start of the day, but because you and the other person both know you have to be at work at a certain time, the meeting tends to be more compact than the traditional business lunch. If you don't want to compete with the morning noise of a restaurant, you can always meet at your office or conference room and deputize someone to bring the doughnuts, bagels, and coffee.

16. Breakfast meetings are also a good way to get to know people. If you select breakfast as the occasion for a first-time meeting, you can achieve three things: 1) You acknowledge that the other person has a busy schedule and that you want to accommodate him; 2) You establish a compact time frame that may help both of you to focus on what needs to be discussed; and 3) You'll almost certainly find that breakfast is cheaper than lunch. If you're on a tight budget, this is no small consideration.

17. For those who work internationally, mornings may be the best time to conduct business with people in different time zones. If you work in New York, for example, getting to work at 8 a.m. gives you three hours to make calls to Europe before their close of business. You are always well advised to schedule your calls as early in the morning as possible—and make sure the people you're contacting know that you'll be calling late in their afternoon. For those working with Asia, the opposite is true: Be ready to stay late and call after your dinner.

18. Whether we admit it or not, most of us are "morning people." Biologically, most folks are more alert during the morning hours than after lunch. If you're planning on a marathon session that could last several hours, requiring every nanosecond of your undivided attention, you are much better off scheduling it for the morning than for the latter part of the day.

19. Burned out by 10:00 am? A second trip to the coffee maker may be just what you need—not so much for the shot of caffeine, but for the change of environment. Just getting up from behind your monitor and leaving your desk behind can help clear your head. You'll be surprised at how a quick change of venue—not to mention a little more oxygen—can refresh your perspective.

20. Try to get most of your major calls out before 10 a.m. Why? Because most meetings are scheduled for 10 or 11 a.m. and then often break for lunch. Starting to call at 10 is more likely to yield "Hello, you've reached the voice mail of . . ." than a live person.

21. You've heard it a million times since you were a kid: Breakfast is the most important meal of the day. Cliché? Doubtless. True? Absolutely. Think about it. If you skip breakfast, odds are the last meal you had was at least twelve hours ago. How can you expect to get your mind and body going if you're running on empty? And make sure you eat a *healthy* breakfast. The energy you get from sugar is quickly burned off, and fats will only slow you down. Your mother (as ususal) was right.

COMMUTING...
DOWN TIME
NO MORE

22. Who said travel time has to be "down time?" If you commute to work on public transportation, such as a bus or subway, this can be an excellent opportunity to catch up on work—or at least on required reading. If you bring files to read, make sure you bring only the ones you need. You don't want to lose files that are critical to your business. Your best bet: create a "traveling folder" where you keep all the papers you're working on at the moment. This way, they stay in one place and are easily accessible.

23. Use the morning commute to help plan the rest of your day. If you manage to grab a seat on the subway, bus, or train, open up your planner and jot down what you need to get done today. This way you can hit the ground running when you get to work. By the same token (so to say), you can use your evening commute to wrap up the day's activities and take stock of what needs to be done the next day.

24. If you read the newspaper on the way to work, consider carrying a pack of moist towelettes. Most newspapers leave the reader with inky hands. The ink can get on your clothes, papers, and reports. Keep the towelettes in your briefcase or purse, and use them so that you won't look like a wreck before the day even begins.

25. Purchase a sturdy portfolio to use as a knee-top desk beneath your papers. Unless your file is thick, you will likely have difficulty writing without a hard back. (And if your file is *that* thick, it will be more cumbersome than you want on a crowded commute.) The portfolio is also an excellent place to put your most sensitive documents. Most portfolios come with a space to put a writing pad. Some include a calculator on the inner cover. Both are great time savers. No portfolio? How about the back of a sturdy attaché?

26. If you drive to work, never try to read while you're driving. Your eyes should be on the road at all times. But being stuck behind the wheel doesn't mean you can't find ways to improve your efficiency. If a great idea comes to you while you're driving, don't let it pass. As soon as you can stop—at a traffic light, say—jot down a note or two. Most auto parts and accessories stores sell paper pads that can be mounted on your dash. But, please, don't start writing until you've come to a complete and safe stop.

27. An even better way to capture fleeting thoughts is with a small hand-held Dictaphone-type recorder. These are not tape recorders, but digital microchip recorders, which can usually store several minutes of reminders. Some of the better models allow you to keep separate "files," so that all your great ideas are logically divided. You can also use a small hand-held tape recorder—but it will be harder to find and retrieve exactly the message you're looking for. Whatever you choose, make certain that you don't have to fumble with the mechanism when you should be driving.

28. If you have a cellular phone in your vehicle, you know how difficult it can be to drive and hold on to the phone at the same time, especially if you throw a stick shift into the bargain. There *is* a solution. Look into "hands-free" phones. Some have special mounts, while others include a microphone positioned in your sun visor. This allows you to talk on "speaker phone" while always looking in the direction that you're going. You get the convenience of a cell phone and the safety of an undistracted view. You still need to exercise caution to ensure that the conversation does not distract you from the harsh realities of the road.

29. If you see that you're going to be stuck in traffic instead of behind your desk, you can use your cell phone to do one of two things. Call into your voice mail to change your message to something like: "Hello, today is the 5th. I will be at work around 10:30 this morning. Please leave me a message." Another option is to call-forward your work number to your cellular number; this way, you'll receive work calls in your car. But do you really want to juggle incredibly irritating traffic and incredibly demanding work?

30. Are you really taking the shortest route to work? Maybe one of the reasons you're not getting to work on time is that you haven't planned your route carefully. At 8:15 on Monday morning, the shortest distance between two points is not always a straight line. Experiment with alternatives. Tune in to the traffic reports on the radio.

31. Consider car pooling. You won't save commuting time, but you may buy work time, including early-morning discussions with your colleagues and coworkers. If nothing else, car-pool conversation gets out of the way the small talk that often adds to first-thing-in-the-morning office inertia.

A *WORKING*
SCHEDULE

32. When was the last time you visited New York? Bet you didn't know it, but the New York City subway system actually runs on a regular schedule. It's not posted for straphangers to see, but it does exist, and most grumbling New Yorkers would be shocked if you told them about it. Anyway, what's the point? Who can the belated commuter hold accountable for a delay? Now you, on the other hand, are held accountable every day—by your clients and customers. By your boss. By your colleagues and coworkers. And by yourself. You owe all of them a schedule, as well as the accountability for sticking to it.

33. Do you have trouble keeping to a schedule? More to the point, do you even have a daily or weekly or monthly schedule? If you don't, and you've managed to survive in the business world, congratulations! You're a lucky member of a very small minority. For the rest of us, though, making and keeping schedules is vital to getting ahead and staying ahead in business.

34. Let's start with the most basic schedule for the typical work day. Plan what you're going to do for the day at the beginning of each day. Plan what you're going to accomplish during the week at the beginning of the week. Here's how to get started: Take out a piece of paper and write down the projects you are working on. Number them in priority order, starting with the most critical projects and working your way down. Now, take out your calendar (or desk-top computer program) and begin plugging in time slots for the most important projects at the *beginning* of the week. If you prefer, divide the time for each project each day, but always give proportionately more time to the critical tasks.

35. Set firm deadlines! *Deadlines?* We're not sure where the word "deadline" came from, but we can hazard a guess . . . and it's not a very pleasant thought. Nevertheless, deadlines work. Remember when you were in college and you knew you were going to be tested on a chunk of material, but you didn't know when? Did you study anyway? Yeah, sure you did. The truth is that only when a firm date for the exam was set did you crack the books. Let's face it, given a choice, we wander down the path of least resistance. With a firm deadline and a little discipline, however, you'd be surprised at all that you can accomplish. Set personal deadlines, write them down, and plan work to meet them.

36. Not a morning person? Can't get your work going at 9 a.m. sharp? Try getting into the office just a little earlier, say 8:45. By the time you've had you're first cup of coffee, checked your e-mail, and said hello to everyone, you're ready to go—and, wonder of wonders, it's 9:00. Plus, it couldn't hurt to have the boss see you at work *before* the start of business.

37. When scheduling a meeting, it's a good idea to avoid times that bump up close to lunch—unless of course you're planning a working lunch. People get antsy late in the morning, or, immediately after lunch, they may resent having had to cut short a meal. Remember, too, that, for most people, the ability to concentrate diminishes significantly by late afternoon, especially on a full stomach.

38. Depending on your relationship with your boss, it may be a good idea to share your schedule with him or her. It shows you're committed to setting goals and keeping them. It also helps you coordinate your activities with the boss's priorities. Even better, set aside some time at the beginning or the end of the week to go over the schedule on a regular basis. Do this even if it's only to show what your priorities are.

39. If you're going to be out of the office, it's always good practice to let the people who work with you know where you'll be and when you'll be back. Here's a tip: Change your voice mail message daily to let people know your schedule and how to reach you.

40. Be realistic when you plan your schedule. Don't expect to produce in a half hour an hour-long presentation on a subject you don't know much about. And don't schedule for yourself more time to work on something you really enjoy, but that you know you could complete in a matter of minutes. Schedule according to needs, not desires.

DESK OR
DISASTER AREA?

41. Let's go back to that guy in the first chapter you just love to hate because he is so organized. Well, let's talk about his desk. I bet you can picture it now. Pencils lined up like wooden soldiers. Phone aligned perfectly. Not a yellow sticky note, memo, or scrap of paper to be found anywhere. Looks nice, but is it the best way to organize? Maybe . . . not.

42. Not every desk has to blind you with its shiny bare surface. All the effort our friend put into making it look neat may not in a pinch help him find what he's looking for. And that's the key to an efficient desktop: functionality—not aesthetics. Your desk is a reflection of you. If you're not a perfectionist by nature, where is it written that your desk has to look perfect?

43. Your computer may claim up to 50 percent of your desk top, leaving you precious little room to work. Try putting the CPU somewhere else. Or, if you have a "tower" model, try placing it on the floor, out of the way—but where you can't kick it, accidentally or otherwise. The extra elbow room may be just what you need to sharpen your edge for efficiency.

44. Still coming in second to your computer in the battle for space? If your budget allows, consider an "L"-shaped desk area. This gives you the benefit of a completely open desk space with no hardware in sight until you make a 45-degree turn to the area dedicated to your computer. This arrangement allows you room for hand work, as well as an uncluttered space for the computer.

45. All that stuff on your desk—do you really need it? Staplers, staple removers, pens, pencils, correction fluid, scissors, computer disks, binders, report folders, dividers, and so on. Consider keeping a lot of this stuff in a drawer or even a storage closet. If you share the closet with others, put your name on the items you value.

46. It's one of the simplest inventions for the office, but it works. Keep your incoming work separated from your outgoing with an old-fashioned in/out stacked box. Getting through to the bottom of the in-box is a very satisfying way of proclaiming, "I've gotten all my work done!"

47. Don't tell us this hasn't happened to you, because it has. You lean over to grab something, and, in a split second, a lake of piping hot coffee materializes across your desktop, drowning papers and everything else in its path. Consider ditching your mug for one of those containers with the spill-proof tops. The cover has the added benefit of keeping your coffee warm, which may mean fewer time-consuming trips to the coffee maker or break room. If you're *really* a klutz, buy a heavy, wide-bottomed cup, which has the stability of an Egyptian pyramid. In any case, remember that beverages and computer keyboards do not go well together.

48. What are the items you need most? A pen for signing letters? A stapler? A letter opener? Be sure to deploy them on the desktop. Then put everything else in your drawer or someplace else. Simplify, simplify, simplify.

49. If you're still having trouble bringing order out of chaos and just can't part with those mountains of papers that put the Himalayas to shame, organize the piles. Create heaps for projects X, Y, and Z. Or divide them into "Due now," "Due soon," and "Long term project" piles. At least you'll have some idea of where to go when you need something, instead of having to scale the peak blindly.

50. Okay, so now you've got one heck of an organized desk. Everything is neat, perfect, and in its place. If there were a black-out, you could *still* find exactly what you need. Just don't let this new look of efficiency erase your personality. Take pride in your desk as an expression of yourself as an individual. Efficiency does not mean you have to remove that picture of your spouse or that great shot of your kids making silly faces. Functionality is important, but so are you, whoever you are.

FILES ARE FOR FINDING

51. If a tree falls in a forest, and no one is there to hear it, does it make a sound? If you can't find a file when you need it, does it exist? Maybe the first question is easier to answer than the second. Files help us not only to organize our work, but our thinking. Keeping well-ordered and well-maintained files is critical to staying ahead in an information-driven economy.

52. To avoid confusion between computer files on diskette or hard drive and hard-copy files in a filing cabinet, make sure the names match. For example, if you save the "Anderson Account" on your hard drive, make sure the label on the file in your filing cabinet says the same thing. This not only helps you, but it helps others, should they need to get to the material in your absence. Also, be consistent. If you say "letters" in one file, don't call them "correspondence" in another. The simpler and more consistent the terms, the easier to remember and the easier to retrieve.

53. Keep only the most active files on your desk throughout the course of the day (unless security is a consideration). Why bother jumping up and down all day to get the same old files?

54. If you want to avoid more clutter on your desk, get a small filing cabinet on wheels. Many of these are attractive and extremely practical. They provide ready access to files, don't clutter up your desk, and they can easily be moved out of the way.

55. Use the reverse pyramid approach. Label files with the most important information first and work down from there: "Anderson Account - Contracts - Building - 1998." This is easy to do on your computer, where you can create main directories and, branching below them, subdirectories. The most recent computer operating systems—such as Windows 95 and Windows 97—allow you to identify files with full names rather than the often cryptic eight-character abbreviations dictated by the DOS operating system. If you do have to abbreviate, whether on the computer or on filing-cabinet labels, make sure your abbreviations are consistent and make good sense.

56. To avoid losing papers, you can punch two holes in the back of a file folder and attach a two-prong clasp. Punch two holes at the top of each document, so that you can safely secure the document to the folder, reducing the chance of papers falling out or becoming dislodged. This method works best when papers are stored in chronological order, with the most recent papers on top and the oldest on the bottom.

57. If your hard drive is starting to clutter up, start archiving old files on other media, such as tape drives, traditional floppy disks, or the new super-capacity diskettes and removable hard drive cartridges that hold up to 100 megabytes and more. If you use appropriate backup software, your archived versions will preserve the basic directory structure intact. As far as data files are concerned, you'll have a mirror image of what was on your hard drive. Make sure you label tapes, diskettes, and cartridges clearly and properly, then store them in a safe place. Keep duplicate back-up files of really important documents, which you should consider storing off-site for added safety.

58. You don't have to be stuck in a hardcopy-only world. Scan hardcopy documents into your computer, and archive the electronic version. The amount of filing space you can save is incredible, and the electronic versions of the files are more easily retrieved. If you don't own a scanner, many copy-service stores—such as Kinko's—offer scanning at per-sheet prices. Here's another idea: fax hardcopy documents to your fax-modem-equipped computer. The result is an electronic image of the document, safe, sound, and conveniently stored on your hard disk. Good computer fax programs also have OCR—"optical character recognition"—programs, which will convert an image file into a format that can be retrieved and modified with your word-processing program.

59. Ah, spring! Warmer weather, beautiful flowers, and the annual ritual of cleaning house. There should be an equivalent rite in the business world. During the spring or any other season—at least once a year—you should sweep through old files, toss out some, archive others, and keep active the remainder. If it takes forever to get through the clutter to find information you need right now, odds are that you are in the habit of hanging on to too many files. Start pruning.

60. Good rule of thumb: If your hardcopy file starts to get more than an inch thick, it's time to divide it. Either reorganize the information by subject (for example, the file for *Anderson Account - Letters* becomes *Anderson Account - Letters - Personal* and *Anderson Account - Letters - Business*), or divide it chronologically. Make sure you label the new files accurately, then go through the original file carefully to make sure you've left nothing behind. You should never have to waste your time by plowing through more than an inch of paper.

GETTING GREATER EFFICIENCY OUT OF OTHERS

61. Getting greater efficiency out of others is the key to successful management. If you've read this far, you already have some ideas about how you can get greater efficiency from yourself. Getting it from others is, frankly, more difficult, but quite possible and well worth doing.

62. Communicate your expectations clearly. "I'm going to need that report by 4 p.m. tomorrow. If we don't have it ready by then we risk losing this account. If you have any questions or concerns, please let me know immediately." You've told the person working on this project in no uncertain terms when it is due. No debate there. But you've also left the door open, so that if there is a problem between now and then, he or she knows to direct questions or comments to you.

63. Plan the work, and work the plan. If you're a boss, sit down with your employee(s) and plan for the month, week, or even just the day ahead. Make sure you are on the same wavelength in terms of which projects have priority, what the deadlines are, and how the tasks should be executed. While no one likes to be talked down to, contrary to what some think, most people crave structure in their lives. Provide a solid framework.

64. People work harder and are more efficient if they see tangible results of their work. Rewards and incentives should be given to people who perform at peak levels. Depending on your company policy, bonuses are effective and universally understood incentives. Even if bonuses are not possible, some form of recognition should be created. Research data indicates that many employees crave recognition even more than they do raises!

65. Assess the person you're working with and adjust accordingly. If you're working with somebody new to the firm, who doesn't know the ropes, you'll probably have to oversee more than you might otherwise. However, be careful to avoid suffocating an employee with too much supervision. Don't cross the line between offering friendly coaching and becoming a mother hen. Remember: "Aid. Don't invade."

66. Hold people accountable. Don't be too understanding or accepting. React honestly if you receive work that is not up to par: "This is not really what we discussed. If you remember, we talked about including item 7-12. What happened?" Be honest, but be polite. Address the issues, not the personalities. For example, avoid saying anything like: "You do this kind of thing all the time! What's wrong with you?" Separate the person from the problem.

67. Suggest solutions. As a manager and even as a colleague, it is your responsibility not only to criticize, but to offer *constructive* solutions to the problems you detect. "I don't think you understood the last assignment. Here are the notes from a meeting I attended that may help clear up the matter. If it's still not clear, let me know, I'll put you in touch with the person who ran the meeting, and he can explain more in detail." Never leave anyone dangling without a line. But while help is a fine thing to offer, it is even better to help the person help himself.

68. When you ask for something to be done, but can't oversee the process, make certain that you leave sufficiently detailed instructions—even if they sound like overkill: "Gary, please send this by Overnight Express to Phil Jones and bill it to the Anderson Account. In case you don't have the address, here it is again . . . " Better to leave a long voice mail message than to return to work and find an important job undone.

69. Information is your most valuable commodity. One way to make people feel closer to what you are doing is to "empower" them by furnishing copies of important memos and other documents. Keep folks "in the loop." Even if there are no action items for everyone all of the time, the fact that you have included them in your "inner circle" gives them a stake in what you value, and it will make it easier to get cooperation at a critical time. Just don't inundate others with a flood of information.

70. One key to successful management is to remember that people are individuals who want to be recognized for their uniqueness. Try to recall certain things about people just to show that you think of them as individuals and not just as "clients" or "employees." If you remember that Bob has a yen for fish, say something like, "You'll love the food today. They're having a special on flounder in the cafeteria." Small talk? You bet. And the smaller the better. This is intimacy without invasiveness, and it says "I know you're an individual, and I pay attention to what you say." Talk about cafeteria flounder may not result in an immediate 50 percent productivity spike, but it will pay off in the long run.

PRODUCTIVE
MEETINGS

71. "Productive meeting" is like the phrase "military intelligence." It strikes you as a contradiction in terms. But please read on. Meetings are meant to accomplish certain tasks. If you wanted to accomplish these tasks on your own, your best course of action would be to plan the work. Since meetings, by definition, involve more than one person, planning is even more important. Before each meeting, draft an agenda. Even if the meeting is between no more than two people, you are better off with a plan than without one. Use any outline format you want: Roman numerals, bullet points, whatever works best. Just put it all down on paper.

72. When putting your agenda together, be sure to place the more important items near the top. Attention wanes as a meeting wears on, and, soon, participants become infected with the MEGO syndrome: "My Eyes Glaze Over." Before the meeting drifts away, get the main business accomplished. Then move on to the less important items.

73. Set a time for a beginning and a time for an end. Of course, everyone needs to know when the meeting will start, but they also should have some idea of when it will end. Although it's sometimes impossible to predict down to exact minute when you'll be breaking up, even an estimate helps. By setting an end time, you send a message that the time for discussion is limited and valuable, and that, therefore, there is no margin for idle chit-chat.

74. Communicate the agenda ahead of time. People like to know what they'll be discussing. Last-minute surprises are rarely appreciated. If you can circulate a draft agenda, do so. If time and space are a problem, consider e-mailing draft agendas to invitees. But be warned: Don't give them the agenda *too* far ahead of time. You run the risk of being flooded with suggestions—or demands—for changes. Besides, circumstances are always evolving, and if you develop an agenda too far in advance, your meeting may be out of date before it takes place. Distribute the agenda no more than one day—or even several hours—before the event.

75. If you're running the meeting, you are responsible for keeping it on track. Although you want to make sure everyone is acknowledged and heard, inevitably there is someone in the room who likes to talk for the sake of filling "dead air." Put an end to this firmly, but diplomatically. Try saying something like, "I hear what you're saying, but maybe it's best if we tackle that at a later date. We've only got a limited time, and we've got three agenda items still to get through."

76. Take notes. Even if everyone is taking their own notes, deputize some one individual to keep minutes. Usually, this task falls to an executive assistant or the most junior person in the room. The notes don't have to be a courtroom-style transcript, but they should accurately summarize what was discussed, with special emphasis on conclusions reached, actions proposed, and issues yet to be resolved. Within a day after the meeting, distribute the notes to all participants. Highlight the action items, so people are reminded of what they are responsible for.

77. Always bring your calendar to meetings. Dates and deadlines are products of most meetings. It is crucial that you flag possible scheduling conflicts. Better to do this at the meeting than have to contact everyone later.

78. Work by consensus. You are much more likely to promote harmony and effective action by working on a consensus basis rather than having constantly to resort to votes or confrontations. If there is strong objection to a course of action, either table the issue for later discussion or ask the objector to make his case. Always give objectors a chance. The lone voice in the wilderness may have something of great value to offer, and, in any case, you don't want anyone to feel railroaded or neglected. But remember, there comes a time when it is obvious how the majority feels, and other business must be attended to.

79. If people in remote locations cannot make it to your meeting, you can include them on the speaker phone or perhaps even through video conferencing. When using a speaker phone, be sure to identify who is talking. If you don't, the remote participant will soon get lost. "This is Bob speaking. I think that . . . " As economical and convenient as speaker phones and video conferencing are, be aware that, for really important meetings—such as getting to know a new client or launching a major project—there is no substitute for face-to-face gatherings. These days, with communications technology so far advanced and readily available, the very fact that you would take the time, trouble, and expense to *travel* to a meeting conveys just how much you value the people with whom you are meeting. High-tech shortcuts work best when the participants are already relatively comfortable with each other.

80. Wrap it up. Before you get to everyone's favorite phrase—"Meeting adjourned!"—you have to bring the session to a close. One of the best ways is to go over the "Action Items" quickly. "Okay, if my notes are correct, Bob will start working on the Grayson report, Sue will contact our contractor in L.A., and John will distribute the report on the Anderson account." This focuses everyone. It is especially effective to keep a separate page of notes for action items. Or highlight action items on your regular notes. Either way, communicate expectations—in black and white, as part of the meeting notes you distribute.

SHOEHORNING
YOUR READING

81. "When am I ever going to have time to read all this?" Whether it's reading newspaper or magazine articles of importance to your work or reading more directly work-related materials, you have to find the time. You can get a lot of your reading done while you commute, if you use public transportation or car-pool. If possible, ease into the day with the lighter reading first.

82. If you want to increase your ability to read more in a given— and limited—amount of time, consider the speed reading option. Maybe you think speed reading is a gimmick at best, a scam at worst. Actually, it works. You can buy a book or two on the subject and teach yourself, or you can investigate professionally taught courses available in your area. You probably won't emerge with an ability to read *War and Peace* in two hours, but you can significantly improve speed, comprehension, and retention skills. Really.

83. If you have a lot of important reading to do but not a lot of time, set aside a span of minutes each morning to plow through your in-box. This is especially important if you must respond to time-sensitive memos or letters at some point during the day. Putting this off can result in missing important deadlines.

84. Bring it home. If you're desperate to catch up, you can create a file that you place in your briefcase to bring home. Use it to transport your reading materials to and from work. If the only time you have is just after you've crawled into bed, so be it. At least you'll make some progress on bringing that pile down to size—and doing so may help you to sleep better.

85. If you can't find a moment to crack open a good business book, be aware that there are a number of companies that offer condensed and digested versions of popular business tomes. They require much less time to read—and getting the gist is better than getting nothing at all. Look in the ad section of major business magazines—or in-flight airline magazines—and you will likely find advertisements for condensed books and condensed book services. Also, several business magazines offer the "best of" other business magazines.

86. Many business books are available on audio cassette, which you can pop into your car's tape player and listen to while commuting or making business calls. Some companies offer condensed versions on audio cassette. These offer verbal summaries of the main points of business bestsellers. No, you're not cheating if you don't actually read words on a printed page. Remember what your other option is—buy the book, but never get around to opening it.

87. If you're a news junky but don't have the time to peruse the paper, the Internet offers all kinds of quick news services. Various wire services are online, as are many major newspapers. You have the added benefit of being able to limit your search to the information you want. You can even set up a "filter" to deliver to you only news likely to be relevant to your business. To streamline the operation yet further, download the pieces, print them up, and read them on the way home.

88. Where is it written that you can't bring back a sandwich to your desk and spend your lunch hour reading? If that's about the only calm moment you have during the day, then take advantage of it. If you can get away from the office to some nice, quiet place, take your lunch and your reading there instead.

89. Prioritize your reading—just as you would prioritize the other tasks you have to get done. Obviously, a memo on a project due in two days should take precedence over a news magazine that you may enjoy, but that won't be of immediate help in doing your job. If you have an in-box on your desk with more than one shelf, use one for urgent and the other for "not so urgent" reading items.

90. Always bring some reading along to meetings you may have outside of the office. Nine times out of ten, your appointment will not see you right away, and you will be asked to wait. Why waste your time reading a well-thumbed, out-of-date copy of some irrelevant magazine when you could be catching up on the memos you couldn't get to earlier? Looking busy in the waiting room also sends a positive signal to the person you're meeting with. Clearly, you believe in creating time, not wasting it.

POWER
BREAKFAST/
POWER LUNCH

91. True, the '80s are behind us, but the "power breakfast" and "power lunch," born of that hard-driving decade, survive. Breakfast can be an excellent opportunity to meet with clients, discuss new ideas, and get to know new faces. If you are the one asking for the meeting, it's a good idea to suggest a place nearby the person you'll be meeting, even if this may be less than convenient for you. If they propose a place closer to you, graciously accept.

92. Eat a little something *before* you go. Yes, it sounds silly, eating *before* breakfast, but if you're going to climb into your car without at least something in your stomach, you are likely to spend the first few minutes sitting with your appointment listening to your stomach growl—not exactly the most favorable impression you can make. Besides, you should give yourself some energy before you get to the main course.

93. You are what you eat. Chowing down on fatty foods like bacon and eggs can slow you tremendously. Sugary foods taste good, but they give you only a temporary boost, and they leave you fatigued. Better stick to healthier food, like oatmeal and grain cereals, which give you natural energy and don't weigh you down.

94. Because breakfast is not a multicourse meal—unlike lunch or dinner—you will likely have to devote less time to eating and have more time for business. This is something to keep in mind when you are deciding whether to meet a client for breakfast or lunch. Be sure to bring along notepads, pens, files, whatever you need. You wouldn't be the first person to ask the waiter for an extra pen.

95. One nice alternative to eating breakfast in a restaurant is to bring the food to the office and eat on the desk or, preferably, in a conference room. The unwritten rule is that the visitor brings the food. Make sure you know ahead of time what the others like, especially if there are any special dietary considerations.

96. Gordon Gecko, the greedy tycoon played by Michael Douglas in the movie *Wall Street*, quipped, "Lunch is for wimps." He was wrong. Lunch is for doing business —albeit in a more relaxed way. Lunch meetings can be an excellent way to get to know another person better and to get some real work done. It's therefore important that you send the right signals. Be sure to suggest a place that is not too dark (so you can at least take notes), not too loud (so you don't have to raise your voice), and neither too expensive nor too cheap. Chances are, you'll recognize a good business restaurant when you see one.

97. If you are used to drinking at lunch time and have no trouble holding your liquor, fine. But if you're going to be conducting serious business and need 110 percent of your concentration, you're much better off going easy on the booze or having none at all. Slurring your judgment is not the best way to make the most intelligent business decisions or the best business impressions. These days, you won't offend anyone by ordering a soft drink. You might even score points for prudence and self-control.

98. When do you pull out the papers? Fancier restaurants frown upon people making their tables into desktops. Enjoy your meal. Engage in some pleasant small talk before getting to the business at hand. You can always get to the bottom line after the main course or during the dessert (if you have any). Remember, power lunches are as much social occasions as they are business occasions.

99. Just like breakfast, lunch is an excellent opportunity to bond with your guests by ordering the meal in your office. If a late-morning client meeting in the conference room is going into overtime, suggest that you order lunch in. Rather than meeting your colleague at a restaurant, offer to meet him or her at their office—you'll bring the food. The gesture signals that you care about their time, and it sets up a more informal atmosphere.

100. It is always a good idea to confirm your lunch appointments on the day of your meeting, especially if you arranged the lunch some time ago. The last thing you want is to show up and find the other person not there. There is nothing wrong with calling up and asking, "We're on for 12 o'clock, right?" It can save you both a lot of time and grief. If you can't reach the person, at least talk to the secretary or leave a voice mail message.

BILLABLE HOURS: TRACKING YOUR TIME

101. If you're in a business where you have to track your time, you already know the importance of keeping accurate records. After all, the old saw "time is money" means just that. With the advent of computers, one of the easiest ways to keep track of hours is by using a contact manager or calendar program. You can quickly record the number of hours or minutes you've worked on a specific project. With most programs, at the end of the month, you can create "filters" that will allow you to print out the hours you worked on a specific project.

102. Know your company's policy—inside and out—on billable hours. Some firms bill in fifteen-minute increments, others smaller, others larger. If you are working in fifteen-minute increments, and you only worked twelve minutes, put down fifteen. No one is expecting you to time your work with the precision of a Swiss watch. But never rip off the client. It's bad business and a bad bargain.

103. Do you count travel time as billable hours? Ordinarily, no. For most white-collar work, it is not considered standard operating procedure to bill someone for the time it takes to get to a particular job. The clock starts ticking the minute you start working on site. If, however, you are flying out to meet a client and you do some work for him at your seat on your laptop/notebook, those are billable hours.

104. The best time to make an entry on a computer time-manager program is just before you start the work. You know already what you're sitting down to do. Also, with that bit of bookkeeping out of the way, you can devote your entire concentration to the task at hand. Once you've completed the project, go back into the program, enter the correct amount of time you spent on that assignment, and then enter your next task.

105. Traveling and don't have a laptop/notebook? In the absence of a computer program, one way to keep central records of the time you worked on particular projects is to use your calendar. Simply record on the appropriate date line the hours and minutes worked, as well as the client for whom the work was done. Calendars that list hours of each day make this task especially easy.

106. When you are choosing contact manager and calendar software programs, make sure the program you select is set up to record billable hours and that it allows you to create filters, so that you can readily print files on individual clients. Also, be sure to buy software that will allow you to calculate the total time on an ongoing basis. Why waste time with accounting after the fact?

107. With billable hours often come expenses for supplies, lunches, transportation, and so on. Always save receipts for *everything*. At the end of the month, when you do invoices, be sure to make photocopies of the receipts for the client. To be extra safe, you might scan your receipts into your computer. If you don't own a scanner, photocopy the receipts and fax the photocopy to your computer fax program. This will give you an electronically archived version for safekeeping and easy access.

108. Set goals and stick to them. At the beginning of each month, either on your own or with your boss, sit down and plan how many hours you should work on each project. Make a list in priority order: the most important tasks should receive the greatest amount of time, the least important should consume the least amount of time. To make sure you're keeping to your goal, periodically check your program to see how many hours you've worked to date. You can check at the end of each week or in the middle of the month. The important thing is to make sure you're on target for the end of the month.

109. If you're responsible for writing up invoices, be sure to be detailed in your descriptions. Nothing is more annoying to a client than to receive a whopping bill for work that is described only in the vaguest of terms. No, you don't have to give a minute-by-minute replay of what was done over a month's time, but if you want to build trust with a client, you will have to demonstrate that you are giving great value for their dollars.

110. If you bring work home and don't have access to your office computer program, you can always remind yourself of how many hours you worked by sending yourself an e-mail message at the office: "Record: worked 3.5 hours on Johnson drilling account," or by leaving yourself a voice mail message. Even if you have the same billable-hours program both at the office and at home, e-mailing a memo may be the better solution. Billable hours information should be recorded in one place only in order to avoid confusion. Unless you're home computer is fully networked to your office machine and its software, it is better to keep everything in one place.

GIVING GOOD
PHONE

111. The phone is one of your most powerful business tools. It is your direct, real-time connection to the outside world. How you project yourself on the phone speaks volumes about you and your company. When answering the phone, it's always a good idea to say your full name: "Bob Jones!" If you answer the phone for calls coming in from the outside, speak clearly, project a positive tone, and convey gratitude to the caller for his call: "Thank you for calling Acme industries. How may I help you?"

112. Though many people say they hate it, voice mail is infinitely preferable to an unanswered phone. Try to keep your voice mail greeting short and to the point: "Hi, you've reached Bill Smith. I'm not at my desk to take your call, so please leave a message. If you need the operator, press zero." You can also get a lot of mileage by changing your voice mail message often. The voice mail greeting is not carved in stone, you know. Consider changing it frequently—even every day. Doing so adds the element of concern and caring that is often missing in recorded messages. "Hi, this is Susan. It's Tuesday, February 4th. I'll be out of the office this morning until 11 o'clock. If you'd like to leave a message for me, please do so after the beep."

113. Can't find a piece of paper to write down your reminders from outside the office? No problem. Just call up your voice mail and leave a verbal reminder for yourself. You've just finished an important lunch meeting and you forgot to bring along a pad. You have to remember to send Bill a copy of the Schultz account, but there's not a pen in sight. Use your cellular phone— or go to a pay phone—call your number, and leave a message to yourself.

114. When leaving voice mail messages, always be sure to say phone numbers s-l-o-w-l-y. Few things are more annoying than having to replay a message repeatedly in order to catch all the slurred digits of a hastily mumbled phone number. If anyone is going to repeat, *you* should: "Please call me be back at 555-1246. Again, that's five-five-five, twelve, forty-six. Thank you." The person on the other end will be grateful.

115. If you ever get stuck in voice mail hell—"Please press one for this department, please press two for that department" and on and on—you are hereby absolved from any guilt if you go ahead and mash the "O" button on your telephone. On most phone systems, this will get you directly to an operator who can send you wherever you want to go. Progress is great, but talking to a live human is often so much easier.

116. Can't find the number for someone or some firm? Dial 411 to find local numbers, or the area code, then 555-1212, for long distance. If you don't know the area code, dial the local operator. In some areas, dialing "00" will get you area code information. Consider bypassing all of this by purchasing any of the incredible CD-ROMs now available that contain the White and Yellow Pages for the entire United States and even for many other countries. These can greatly speed up any phone search. You can easily look up numbers by name, by location, or by business type.

117. Make use of your phone's speed-dial feature to program your most frequently called numbers. Putting in the number the first time takes minimal effort, and this is a real time saver.

118. Your phone company offers some excellent features that allow you to conduct your business more efficiently. If you need to have a phone conversation with two people in different locations, three-way calling allows all three of you to speak at the same time. Call-waiting signals you that you have another incoming call. And call-forwarding allows you to route calls directly to an alternate number when you are out of the office.

119. Know when to get off the phone. Serious business conversations should not last any longer than they have to. Pleasantries are exchanged early on, and then it's down to business. Don't mix too much personal commentary with your business conversation. Keep it on a professional level.

120. Try not to let the phone ring more than three times before answering. Answering it after the first ring may come across as over-eagerness or suggest that you really don't have much else to do. Answering it after the second ring is about right. Let it ring more than three or four times, however, and you risk losing the call. If you're completely swamped, and you've got exactly two minutes to finish a project, yes, it is okay to let the call bounce into voice mail. Remember: the phone works for you; you don't work for the phone.

KEEPING
APPOINTMENTS

121. Meetings outside your office are an important part of doing business. A premium is placed on making the right impression, and no one has never made the right impression by showing up late. Do whatever you must to materialize on time. Three o'clock means 3:00, not 3:10. Your goal is complete punctuality.

122. When setting up appointments over the phone, always repeat the information you've written down: "Let me just read that back to you—that's 4 p.m. in suite 1256 at 356 Madison Avenue. Is that correct?" Double checking eases your mind. Make sure you also double check their phone and other contact numbers.

123. If you've planned an appointment well in advance, it may be a good idea to call on the day of the appointment to reconfirm. You may not even have to speak to the person you're meeting. A secretary or executive assistant should be fine. Calling in is not only a courtesy, it may reveal that the other person has changed his plans and has neglected to tell you. You'll save yourself time— and the other person embarrassment.

124. Give yourself plenty of time, especially if you work in a city where traffic congestion is a problem. It is much better to allow an excess of time and arrive early than late. Use any extra minutes to relax, clear your head, collect your thoughts, or even catch up on an odd bit of reading. Most important, you'll go into the meeting without being rushed, distracted, or cursed by the stigma of tardiness.

125. If you arrive early at an unfamiliar destination, take advantage of the extra time to familiarize yourself with the building. Find out exactly where you have to go. Avoid last-minute panic. There's nothing wrong with getting off the elevator, confirming that you have the correct floor, then getting back on the elevator and coming back for your appointment twenty minutes later.

126. But when, exactly, *should* you arrive? There are different schools of thought on this subject. If your appointment is in the early morning, try to arrive as close to the appointed time as possible. If you arrive too early, you may intrude on your host's morning routine and throw her off schedule. If you're going to an appointment where you will likely be waiting in a reception area, arriving four or five minutes early is perfectly acceptable. This gives the person you're meeting with time to prepare, and it is generally understood that you'll be waiting. What else is a reception area for?

127. If you're giving directions on how to get to your office or to another meeting place, be as detailed and as clear as possible. Provide landmarks to help guide the way: "We are directly across the street from the Hilton and right next to the Exxon building. When you go into the lobby, turn left at the blue reception desk and take the elevators to the 5th floor." The result of a meeting should be a solution to a problem. The first "problem" in any meeting is getting to the meeting place. Start off right by providing a crystal clear solution to this problem first.

128. If you are giving directions to somebody who will be visiting your town for the first time, be sure to give directions relative to their arrival point: the airport, train station, whatever. Another good idea is to fax them a map of the city in advance and circle the address of the meeting place.

129. Use the alarm function on your computer contact manager program to alert you to impending appointments. Give yourself plenty of time to prepare for appointments outside of the office and relatively less time for appointments you are hosting. If the appointment is scheduled for first thing in the morning, set the alarm for the end of the day before.

130. If you or the person you're meeting has a cellular phone, make sure you have the numbers handy. If you're stuck in traffic, and it's obvious you're not going to make it on time, call your appointment. Let her know the situation and give her a revised ETA (estimated time of arrival). If you don't have a cell phone, try using a pay phone. If necessary, ask the taxi driver to pull over and wait while you use the pay phone. The important thing is to keep your appointment informed.

TRAVELING

131. Business trips can be incredibly productive times. If you don't already have a laptop or notebook computer and are planning on doing a lot of business out the office, why not invest in one? It will allow you to bring virtually all of your work with you.

132. Recharge your laptop/notebook batteries the night before your trip. Many airlines also offer electrical outlets for users of portable computers, but don't count on their being available. Always follow the airline's instructions on when you can and cannot use your machine. There have been reports of electronic devices interfering with aircraft navigational systems. Getting work done is fine, but it's also important to reach your destination in one piece!

133. Store important documents in your carry-on luggage only. If you've ever had an airline lose your luggage — and it happens to thousands of people every day—you will know better than to risk your important work by putting it in checked luggage. Most airlines let you take two carry-ons. One bag should contain work, the other at least one change of clothes and your toiletries. Even if your checked bags go astray, you'll still be able to look presentable.

134. Before traveling overseas, research your destination country extensively. Know the visa requirements, voltage for electric appliances, the major holidays, where to exchange money, and so on. Spend extra time reviewing important business customs and courtesies. For example, presenting your business card is practically a ceremonial event in Japan, and a Japanese businessperson will take offense if you instantly slip the proffered card into your pocket with barely a glance. The more you know in advance, the better prepared you will be when you hit the ground. Much of this information today is available on the Internet. Individual countries have their own Web sites, and the U.S. Department of Commerce has individual country reports at **http://www.ita.gov**, which offer a wealth of information to the international business traveler. For domestic travelers, most states now have Web sites that also offer much of value. Use search engines such as **http://www.yahoo.com** to get started.

135. If you're traveling great distances, consider the first and the last days as travel days only. Jet lag is very real, and it can hit you with the fatiguing force of a bad cold or the flu. It is a much better idea to arrange your first appointment the day *after* you arrive. This gives you a chance to get some rest, freshen up, shower, and be ready to go to work.

136. Most major hotels have business centers that often feature secretarial services, computers, printers, faxes, scanners, and other professional amenities. Bear in mind that the services can be pricey, but they are an excellent option for the busy business traveler. If necessary, compromise to cut down on costs. For example, bring along your laptop/notebook rather than paying to use the business center's computers, but go ahead and make use of the center's printer rather than packing your own portable printer.

137. Bring along an alarm clock or a portable radio with an alarm. Although it's a good idea to leave a message with the reception desk for a wake up call, you cannot rely 100 percent on that call getting made. Oversleeping is a real hazard, especially if you're jet lagged. Adopt a belt-and-suspenders approach by using an alarm clock as well as a wake up call.

138. Keep a file for expenses. It doesn't have to be fancy—a regular business envelope will do—but make sure that it is separate from your other papers and that you dump every receipt into it. Eager to get your expenses sorted out? Skip the in-flight movie on the way home, and organize your expense report instead.

139. If you have an e-mail account, call your service provider and ask for the local access numbers you'll need to use when traveling. Be sure to write down access numbers. Better yet, save the numbers in your dial-up and label them appropriately. This way you're only a click away from checking on your electronic mail.

140. Before you go, make sure people know how to contact you. Leave an informative message on your voice mail: "Hi. You've reached Bill Smith. Between April 3 and 8, I will be in our Chicago office at (800) 555-7675. If you wish to speak to my executive assistant, please press zero. Or, if you prefer, leave a message after the beep. I will be checking my messages regularly." Give a copy of your schedule, travel itinerary, and contact numbers to important colleagues and assistants.

NETWORKING

141. If you're in the kind of business where you constantly meet people and network, you already know there is an almost formal ritual to the process. And the ritual begins with the business card. Before attending a meeting or conference, always be sure to bring plenty of business cards. To show up without them is far more "uncool" than to show up with more than enough.

142. In addition to your name, title, address, phone, and fax, you should also put your e-mail address on your business card. E-mail is fast becoming the preferred means of business communications. Let them know how to reach you.

143. Although everyone feels silly wearing them, name tags at group events are a terrific help. They help you put a name to a face, and if the company name is listed on the tag, you are also provided with an excellent entrée to a conversation: "Oh, I see you work for Johnson & Miller. I hear they're a great company to do business with." It's expected that the subject of who you are and what you do will come up very early in a conversation. However, bringing it up tactfully can take practice.

144. Business cards are meant to be reminders of how to get in touch with you. It's not a good idea to hand them out indiscriminately. They lose their value that way. If you have struck up a conversation with someone interesting enough to warrant someday continuing the conversation, then you should exchange cards. If someone seems like a good business prospect, exchange cards. But giving them out like party favors is bad form.

145. If you are planning to work overseas or are going on an overseas business trip, it might be a worthwhile investment to have your card translated on the reverse side. This shows savvy, sophistication, and a high degree of cultural sensitivity.

146. How do you follow up on a meeting? It is a good idea to reinitiate the contact by sending an e-mail or a regular letter not too long after the first meeting. Make reference to the meeting in your first paragraph. If you hit it off very well, and it seems like you have an informal rapport with the person, skip the written message and go right to a phone call.

147. Name names. There's nothing wrong with saying, "Oh, you work there? Do you know Bob Reginald?" People trust people more when they know people you know. Familiarity is comforting. But be careful, no one likes an obvious name dropper, and the point of a conversation is to find out more about each other, not spend all your time figuring out who you know in common.

148. At a social-business gathering, don't stay with one person too long. Usually, you want to meet as many people as possible who can potentially be of use to you. It's expected that you will circulate throughout the course of the event. Besides, the other person will want to circulate as well, and by monopolizing him or her, you may be creating an uncomfortable situation.

149. Make a habit of going through your cache of collected business card frequently and entering the names and contact numbers into your contact manager as soon as possible. You might consider purchasing one of the new business card scanners now on the market, which will send business card information directly into your computer. This way, if you lose the card, at least you'll have a copy in an electronic file. Some business cards can be saved in books, which you can arrange alphabetically. There are also Rolodex-like devices that allow you to punch the bottom of the card, so it can be placed directly in your address card file. No transcribing is necessary.

150. Most of us meet a number of people at an event, dutifully secure their business cards, then forget who they were a day, week, or month later. One way to avoid this trap is to write—directly on the reverse side of the card—something about them or the conversation you had: "Spoke re problems setting up factories in SE Asia." Whatever you jot down should serve as a quick reminder that will allow you to remember with whom you spoke and why. Usually, it's best to scribble this information soon after the event rather than during it. You don't want to appear predatory.

DELEGATING

VERSUS DOING

151. Management today moves at a pace unheard of only a few years ago. More than ever before, time is of the essence, and there are ways to maximize your time by delegating work instead of overburdening yourself. Before the start of a project, always figure out the time necessary to complete the task. Work backward: assume the project is finished and add up what it has taken to complete it. If there are aspects of the project that are simply going to take too much of your time, you are much better off farming out the work than tying yourself down. Delegate to those employees who have the necessary skills, have the time, and can meet the deadline.

152. Temping is one of America's growth industries. As companies continue to downsize, the demand for temps burgeons. One of the most cost-effective ways to complete projects on time and within budget is to bring on temporary help for specific tasks, especially in areas where you or your staff may lack expertise. There are no long-term commitments, and there are temps for virtually every task—from the highly technical to non-skilled work.

153. One of the best ways to get quality temps is through a reputable agency. There are dozens of temp agencies, many of them with offices all around the country. Interview a few to get an idea of what type of personnel they have available. Check their references and follow up on at least some of them. If you don't know where to start, check your local Yellow Pages or contact National Association of Temporary and Staffing Services, in Alexandria, Virginia, at 1(703) 549-6287.

154. One of the best times to delegate work is at meetings when specific projects are being discussed. This allows you to lay all your cards on the table: "Jan, you're in charge of lay-out. Bob, I want you to do the editing." Waiting until after a meeting to delegate specific work assignments invites trouble. People may wonder why you waited. Were you hiding something? Were you showing favoritism? Besides, it's simply easier to coordinate the schedules of several people if you have them all assembled at one place and at one time.

155. Check in midway through a project to see what progress is being made. Just don't be too pushy. *Wrong:* "So when is that assignment going to be on my desk?" *Right:* "I know you're busy, but I just wanted to check in and see how that project's coming along." Always give people breathing space. If you trust the person to get the assignment done, you'll likely get the best results by resisting the temptation to get too involved. Give the person the opportunity to claim "ownership" of the project, to make it his own.

156. One of the great advantages to e-mail is that assignments can be parceled out to people who physically work in remote locations. You no longer have to hand out assignments only to people work nearby. Writing, artwork, spreadsheets—whatever—can now be executed by people inside and outside your organization, working down the block or across the country. Arguably, it does become somewhat harder to manage in the absence of the "personal touch," but the gains in time saved and expertise exploited usually far outweigh this consideration.

157. When using a temp worker, it is always a good idea to audition him with some minimally critical assignments to test his skill level. You would not want to hand an untried temp your most sensitive project first. Better to start off slowly, then work up to the level you desire. This may cost some money in the short run, but it is so much insurance against potentially damaging mistakes in the long run.

158. Set reminders in your contact manager program to check in on people working for you. It's hard enough keeping track of your own work, but managing others is even more of a challenge. One way to keep track is to write in your calendar when assignments are due and when is the best time to check in on progress. On some computer programs, you can even set audio alarms that will alert you. Set up these checkpoints at the beginning of a project, or you may just never get around to it.

159. When delegating work, be clear about your expectations. Set firm deadlines. And if you feel it's appropriate, talk with people individually about what you have specified. "I know you've never done anything like this before, but I feel you're ready for this type of assignment." Or "I think you can do better than that last report. I know you'll try harder this time."

160. Make it a rule: When attending a meeting, everyone must not only bring a notepad to take notes, but must also bring their calendars (or notebook computers, if that's where they keep their calendar). Make sure everyone marks down what they have to do and when it's due. This way there's no more "Oh, I forgot." Proactively avert time conflicts by making sure everyone involved understands the time commitments involved.

SHARPENING YOUR SKILLS

161. Recent statistics suggest that most folks will change jobs at least ten times during their working lives. The implications of this are far reaching. True, we have more variety in our professional lives than previous generations enjoyed, but we must constantly learn more to keep our edge. One way to know what is expected of you is to go back to your present job description—if you have one. Better yet, find the job description for the higher position you'd *really* like. Do you have what it says it takes to do the job? What skills are you missing? This exercise is not meant to depress or intimidate, but to help you realistically assess where you are and where you have to get to.

162. Need to sharpen computer skills? The best place to learn is on the job, but don't let that cut into your productivity time. If you can afford the software, buy a copy for yourself and try learning it at home. This kind of practice will help in your daily work.

163. If you are interested in learning special computer skills such as the Hyper-Text Mark-up Language (HTML) used in publishing Internet Web sites, there are a number of books that come complete with disks or CD-ROMs to get you started. The same is true for books covering other computer programs and computer programming languages. Also, many private and public colleges and universities offer extension courses devoted to general and specialized computer skills. The courses are not always cheap, but they can be an invaluable investment that will give you an edge in the employment marketplace.

164. Perhaps the time has come to learn a foreign language. In our global economy, language skills can be extremely useful. There are a variety of ways to acquire or sharpen language skills. Most bookstores stock foreign language training books, many of which come with cassette tapes or CD-ROMs. Also, many cities have language institutes that specialize in this kind of program. If you can't find any, you might try calling the language department of your local college or university. They may recommend their own classes, a separate institution, or give you the names of qualified graduate students who can tutor you.

165. If you haven't visited the career section of your local bookstore or library, do so soon. There is a wealth of information on sharpening skills in a variety of fields. Many of the books include "workbook" sections that allow you to test your current knowledge and score yourself.

166. Set aside time each day to practice skills you are trying to acquire. Studies have repeatedly shown that it is better to practice a musical instrument—or any other skill—a little each day rather than for a long time once a week. Repetition is key. Work out a schedule that will allow you some time—preferably every day of the week—to try out your skills. Develop the discipline to stick to your schedule.

167. Talk to your boss or to your human resources department to find out if your company will help pay for special training. If the skills you need are directly related to your job and will clearly make you a better employee, you should be able to put together a persuasive case for funding.

168. Check out the Internet. Depending on the type of skills-improvement you're looking for, odds are that there is a site on the Internet that can help you to define what you're looking for and perhaps even get you started. Be sure especially to look for "FAQs," or "Frequently Asked Questions." They provide plain-English answers to a variety of basic questions in a given field.

169. Keep abreast of what skills are prized or required these days. With change happening in the blink of an eye, it's possible that the skills you learn today will become useless in a year or less! It's very important that you keep up to date on what constitutes the cutting edge in your industry. You can get much of this information from industry newsletters, professional journals, professional associations, and by attending skills-related conferences, seminars, and training sessions.

170. If you are an independent contractor and don't have a big company name to trumpet your reputation, one of the best ways to advertise your skills is to sell yourself on your business card: "Bob Jones, Jones & Co., Mechanical Engineering, 50 Maple St., etc." This is especially important when the name of your firm— Jones & Co.—offers no clue as to what you do. While you're at it, how about a single line of out-and-out advertising—also right on card? For example, add to the Jones card: "The HVAC Experts."

HIGH TECH TO THE RESCUE

171. We've already looked at a number of high-tech solutions to everyday business challenges. This chapter offers yet a few more helpful ideas. If you are accustomed to faxing the same document to a number of people, there are easier ways to get this done than standing in front of the fax machine all day. If you have fax software on your computer, you can program it to send the faxes after business hours. Simply set the time you'd like it to start sending, go home, and let the machine do its work for you.

172. Frustrated by a piece of software that doesn't seem to work the way it's supposed to? When you purchase a new piece of software, take advantage of whatever customer support comes with the package, and if the vendor offers additional customer support for a fee, it's usually a good idea to pay for it. True, it is sometimes difficult getting through to a busy customer support desk, but it is usually worth the wait, since, oftentimes, the technician can solve your problem right on the phone. Some systems even allow the tech support people to tap into your computer and make changes remotely. Before resorting to tech support, however, read the manual, look at any "read me" files that are included on the software's installation disks or CD-ROM, and check out the company's Web site on the Internet. Here you'll find detailed product information and FAQ sheets that can sometimes answer your questions.

173. If you have to make a presentation with slides, consider renting or buying a data projector, which will allow you to take whatever is on your computer screen and project it onto a wall or screen for all to see. This can be especially useful for presentations in small rooms. It's a great way to move beyond the deadly dull click-and-look rhythm of the traditional slide projector presentation.

174. Depending on the type of program you're running, a data projector can allow you to show still images as well as moving images, *and* combine these with sound. This can really spice up a presentation and will certainly tell your audience that you're on the cutting edge.

175. Keep duplicates of your back-up files. Whether you use a Zip® drive, a SyQuest® disk, a tape drive, or plain old floppies, it is always a good idea to keep two copies on file, preferably in different places, one of which should be remote from your computer. That way, if your hard drive fails—and someday, unfortunately, it will—and you lose data, you'll have a back-up. If you suffer loss through fire, flood, or theft, you'll still have the remote backup.

176. There are cheap ways to update software. If you are using software programs that are fairly old, be sure to look for upgrades. Many software companies offer upgrade discounts to people who have purchased previous versions. Also, check out each companies' Web sites. Many firms offer upgrades for free or at a nominal cost.

177. If you are in the market for a new computer, printer, or peripheral, one of the best ways to shop is to talk to computer-literate friends about what they use. Often, you will find out from them a great deal more than just what an item costs. You should also read a few of the many personal computer magazines that are available not just in computer stores, but on most larger newsstands. These are rich in ads, prices, and equipment and software tests and reviews.

178. If you have the disk space, it is a wise practice to retain older versions of the computer programs you use. If you are working with someone who does not have the latest software, you may need the older program to ensure 100 percent compatibility with the other person's data. Some newer programs are not fully "backward compatible"—that is, they may not allow you to view, edit, or save documents created by earlier versions of the software.

179. Just as you need periodically to clean out your filing cabinets, it's a good idea occasionally to clean out your computer files. If you notice you're running low on hard drive space, now is the time to start pruning files you don't need. If you don't know where to begin, you can at least create a list by asking the computer to run a search for files with specific extensions. For example, if you use a PC and write a lot of Microsoft Word® texts, you can search for all files with the extension ".doc." This will yield a list that you can then arrange by name, date created, size, and so on. Start cleaning out the ones you know you definitely don't need. If you can't remember which is which, click on the file to open it up and review the materials on screen to decide whether to keep it or not. You don't have to consign discarded files to oblivion. Consider making archive copies on a Zip® drive, a SyQuest® disk, a tape drive, or on floppies; then remove the files from your hard drive.

180. It's always a good investment to buy a diagnostic program, especially if one was not bundled with the computer when you purchased it. Such a program helps you pinpoint specific hardware and software problems and solve them without having to resort to outside help.

181. If you do a lot work on the Internet, routinely get e-mail, or use disks from others, better regularly run a good antivirus program. Computer viruses are real and can do real damage to your computer or network—possibly to the tune of thousands of dollars. The better antivirus programs offer biweekly or monthly updates, available by mail on diskettes or in downloadable form from the World Wide Web or an FTP site on the Internet. If you've ever had a virus problem, you know how valuable an antivirus program can be.

HOMEWORK

182. Good heavens, after so many years of school, you mean I *still* have to do homework? If you're like most business people these days, you at least occasionally need to bring some of your work home with you. One way to organize your "homework" better and save time is to carry everything on computer disks and skip the paper altogether. Be sure to avoid confusion over what version of a file you have by marking the disk with some phrase that will make sense to you, like "transfer disk."

183. If you have a computer at home, it is always a good idea to have on your hard disk the program or programs you use at work. This way, you will have no trouble transferring and working on documents, and you won't have to deal with converting documents produced by one program or version for use with another. Be careful, though. It is usually illegal simply to copy the program from your work computer to your home computer. You will need to purchase—or have your company purchase for you—a separate program for use on your home machine. Software piracy is a serious crime.

184. Once you've finished work on a document at home, always be sure to date it, so that you can keep track of which version is the current one. For example, you could write "Version 1.2 as of April 30, 1997." Remember to delete this line when you're ready to print out your final presentation copy.

185. Bring home only the files you need—and pare even these down, especially if you are dealing with hard copy. If you're worried about mixing up different documents from different files, write the name of the file lightly in pencil at the top margin, so you'll know where it came from.

186. If you get confused about which computer file from home should replace the old file at work, look for the file with the latest date. The latest-dated file will have the most recent changes.

187. Sometimes the best times to work at home are in the really off-hours. Just because you're working doesn't mean you shouldn't enjoy your life. Depending on your sleeping habits, it may be better to get that homework done early in the morning or just before you go to bed rather than right after you get home. Heed your internal clock, and see what works best for you.

188. Reading makes for good homework. Some offices are so hectic during the day that there's simply no opportunity to sit back and read your memos and papers. In an aggressively busy office, you may even feel guilty about taking time to read. In a home setting, however, you should feel free of guilt and comfortable enough to think, to plan expansively, or simply to put things in priority order.

189. Set limits. If you know that, in an ordinary workday, 5 p.m. is quitting time, set a reasonable quitting time at home. In order to structure your work outside of the office, set a deadline for yourself by establishing precisely when you want to start and when you want to finish. You may not always keep to it, but at least you'll have an idea of when it's time to get started and, even more important, when it's time to quit. This should help motivate you to get your work done—and relieve you of guilty feelings when you put your laptop or notebook computer away for the evening.

190. If you have kids in the house, it can be a good idea to ask them to help you with some simpler projects, such as organizing files. If they're older, try asking them to do basic online research for you. If you haven't realized it by now, kids are more comfortable with a computer than most adults are. Securing such help can take a lot of the sting out of working at home. It lets your children feel helpful, and it's a great bonding experience, as well as an introduction for them to the world of work and responsibility. Just make sure you let them stop when it ceases to be fun.

191. Don't overload yourself. If you're already bushed from a hard day in the office, don't burn yourself out completely by continuing the same grueling pace at home. You may end up with what economists call "diminishing marginal returns." In other words, the harder you try, the less you achieve. If you feel the approach of burnout, get up and—literally—walk away from your work. Weather permitting, go out and take a walk. Smell the roses. Clear your head.

JUST IN CASE...

192. Job security is a thing of the past. For increasing numbers of us, the day arrives when we've been downsized, sent into early retirement, or offered a severance package we can't refuse. Always keep a current résumé on hand. Keep it up to date. When you finish a project of which you are particularly proud, be sure to add it as a new line in your résumé. You might even want to keep a list of accomplishments separate from your formal résumé. This allows you to create a "laundry list" of items from which you can pick and chose to tailor résumés to individual recipients.

193. Never keep a copy of your résumé on your office computer. Always keep it at home. The last thing you want is for anyone at work to find you working on a résumé. It will send an irretrievable signal that could cost you your job. Take time to create and maintain your résumé at home.

194. As you meet people throughout the course of your career, always keep in the back of your mind the possibility that you may want to work with or for that person some time in the not-too-distant future. Maintain your business card and business contact file, and be certain to treat with respect all those with whom you come into contact. What goes around comes around.

194. When putting together a résumé, it is a good strategy to start with a section labeled "Skills." Because people reviewing résumés tend to browse through a pile of them at a time, you need to draw attention to the information that really sells you. Save your potential employer time by telling him up front what you can do.

196. If you are in an industry burdened by a history of downsizing, investigate what options there are for you to go out on your own, even if it's only as a temporary measure. Be prepared. In fact, many people find they make more money on their own than in full-time service to others. There may be no single easy way to get the lowdown on the free-lance or independent operator scene in your field. But speak informally and frequently to people who are already out on their own. Just be careful that your conversations don't betray fear for your job. You could wind up sending signals that create a self-fulfilling prophecy.

197. If you do decide to go out on your own, bear in mind you'll be taking on responsibilities you never had to deal with before. You will likely find that you are better off subcontracting accounting, tax, and other responsibilities to others rather than letting these functions eat up all your time. Better to pay for it and get it done right, than to let it consume the time you need to obtain business and perform for your clients.

198. Compile and maintain a list of people who can help you, should you find your job suddenly in jeopardy. Candidates for the list include folks who have an inside track on who's hiring and how to get to them.

199. Another list you should create and maintain is the names of references on whom you can *really* count. These are people who will vouch for you, should you need to change jobs. Candidates include ex-bosses, colleagues, and friends who are familiar with your work. It's a good idea to keep these people up-to-date on what you're doing. When it comes time to get a letter of reference, don't be shy about *telling* your references what you would like them to say. Ask them to focus on specific projects and accomplishments rather than general appraisals of competence and character.

200. To the degree that it is possible, save your best work on disk. You will want to be able to show writing and other samples to prospective employers. Create and maintain a specific file just for this purpose. If a certain disagreeable substance ever hits the fan, you want to be able to hit the ground running. The "best of" file should be a work-in-progress, compiled as you complete each project. You don't want to have to try to pull things together from a dozen half-forgotten sources at some anxiety-pressed eleventh hour.

201. Use the Internet to scout out help-wanted ads. Many newspapers now publish general help-wanted sections online, and you should also search for the Web sites of specific companies and other organizations, which often announce open positions over the Net. Even if you're not yet actively looking for a new job, monitoring the Internet will give you an idea of what kind of opportunities are out there, and what kind of salaries are being offered. You'll also find a variety of Web pages created by self-employed people, which may enhance your picture of the opportunities in your field. Some online service providers, such as CompuServe℠, have professional "chat rooms," where people get together to discuss all kinds of job-related issues. You may find that such forums provide a window into how others prepare themselves for career advancement and career change—voluntary or not.